BUILDING JOB SKILLS™

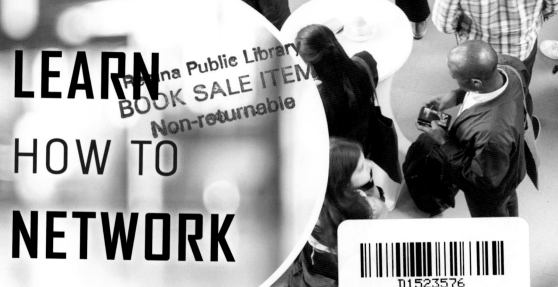

LEARN
HOW TO
NETWORK

D1523576

Elissa Thompson and Greg Roza

Rosen
YA™

New York

Published in 2020 by The Rosen Publishing Group, Inc.
29 East 21st Street, New York, NY 10010

Copyright © 2020 by The Rosen Publishing Group, Inc.

First Edition

Library of Congress Cataloging-in-Publication Data

Names: Thompson, Elissa, author. | Roza, Greg, author.
Title: Learn how to network / Elissa Thompson and Greg Roza.
Description: New York : Rosen Publishing, 2020 | Series: Building job skills |
Audience: Grade level 7–12. | Includes bibliographical references and index.
Identifiers: LCCN 2019008670| ISBN 9781725347168
(library bound) | ISBN 9781725347151 (pbk.)
Subjects: LCSH: Vocational guidance—Juvenile literature. | Business
networks—Juvenile literature. | Career development—Juvenile literature.
Classification: LCC HF5381.2 .T46 2020 | DDC 650.1/3—dc23
LC record available at https://lccn.loc.gov/2019008670

Manufactured in the United States of America

CONTENTS

INTRODUCTION

1t's all about who you know.

It's time to start looking for your first job. Or maybe the gig you had last summer isn't working out any longer. Perhaps you're ready to talk to some people about college or a major you've been considering. Or maybe you just want to know how to answer your aunt when she corners you at Thanksgiving to ask what you're going to do with your life.

So how should you go about finding the answers to some of these questions? Networking.

You might think networking is just for adults, people in business suits awkwardly holding plates of cheese while they trade business cards. But this is not the case! Networking can work for you, right now, to help you get started on your career.

Take Lauren Castro. She tried for a long time to get a job, without any success. "I applied to about 30 companies—fast-food, Target, Sports Chalet," she told Alina Tugend at the *New York Times*. Despite scoring a few interviews, she wasn't having much luck. Instead of a job offer, she kept getting "the inevitable email saying they hired someone with more experience. I was tired of getting email after email saying I needed experience when I couldn't get it."

So how did Castro finally land a gig? She used her network. She got a job at a local pizzeria because her sister's soccer coach knew the owners.

You might not realize it, but you are connected to so many different people. Find your network, and you can start on a career path today.

Using that kind of connection is called networking. By utilizing who you know, who they know, and who you can get to know, you'll be able to learn more about potential careers, hear about job opportunities, and help connect others as well.

Networking isn't just about finding a job. It's about building a support system of people who will follow you throughout your life. You'll assist each other in achieving goals, creating new opportunities, and

By establishing connections and reaching out to others, you can begin to build an amazing career.

"The best networking comes out of genuine relationships," Lara Zielin told Anna Cooperberg at Teen Vogue. "If you're listening to people and you're genuinely interested in what they have to say and what they're doing, you can ask good questions and get to know them," Zielin said. By being true to yourself, you can grow your network organically and without too much awkward small talk.

While networking might sound like an overwhelming task, it is definitely possible that you're further along in establishing your own network than you might think. And there's good news, all your social media savvy can only help you. Although adults might not know the ins and outs of Twitter or when it's the right time to comment on an Instagram post (as in, right away, not three months later), you're already set up to engage with contacts and companies online.

Learn how to brainstorm who is in your network already and how it can grow even further. Find out tips and tricks on how to approach people, what to say, and how to leverage your online presence, all to make an amazing first impression. It's time to take charge of your career.

Time to get networking!

WHAT IS A NETWORK, ANYWAY?

A network may sound like something only adults have, but teens definitely are part of networks, too. Your family and friends want to help you succeed. All you have to do is think critically about who can help you—and then speak up.

THE IMPORTANCE OF NETWORKING

What exactly is networking? It's building up a treasure trove of people and resources who can someday help you achieve new goals. Have a problem? Ready to tackle a new career challenge? Having strong network connections in place will help you conquer obstacles and achieve new goals.

You may pride yourself on being independent, but you can't do everything yourself. A well-tended network can help you achieve your goals in countless ways. Your network may certainly help you get a job. But it might also be about finding someone to set up an e-tailer site to sell your jewelry, to track down that

Think about who you know. Then think about who they know. These are your network connections. By maintaining relationships and asking questions, you can grow these relationships and make them work for you.

rare baseball card you've been looking for, or to find someone to housesit while you and your family are on vacation. Or you might just get someone smart to talk to when you need advice.

Whether you want to be a mechanic, a botanist, a carpenter, or a teacher, a network can be a guiding force in your professional career. Getting a job after you graduate can sound like a difficult process, but it doesn't have to be. Use your networking skills to make your job search more productive. By making it a point to meet new people and use already established

Consider what type of job you might enjoy. Then ask around to find out who you know who is established in that career. Make a connection.

contacts, you'll be able to open doors you never knew were there.

USING THE NETWORK YOU HAVE

Consider this example. Clark is a high school senior, about to graduate. He likes science and math and is attending a vocational school for his senior year to learn basic electrician skills. He isn't 100 percent sure what he wants to do with these skills, but he does know that college isn't right for him. His dad suggests he talk to his cousin Blair, who manages an electronics store. Blair explains to Clark that after working as a clerk for two years, she is now in management. She's using her salary to pay for college. She offers to recommend Clark for the next job opening at the store. Clark fills out an application.

In the meantime, Clark keeps mowing lawns in his neighborhood, something he has been doing for more than three years. He earns $40 a lawn, which gives him enough spending money for the weekend. However, Clark knows he doesn't want to mow lawns forever. On Thursdays, Clark mows Mr. MacReady's lawn. Mr. MacReady informs Clark that he can get him a job interview with a friend of his who owns a coffee shop.

A few weeks later, Clark interviews for both jobs. He makes a good impression on both employers and is offered both jobs. Clark decides to take the job in the electronics store; he figures it will best help him to decide how he wants to use the skills he learned in vocational school. Now that Clark has taken the job, however, there is no one to mow Mr. MacReady's lawn.

You are connected to so many more people than you think. By being smart about who you know, you can grow your network efficiently and effectively.

To return the kindness Mr. MacReady showed him, Clark puts him in touch with his friend Gary.

Clark made good use of his network of friends and family to increase his chances of finding a job. Gary and Mr. MacReady also benefited from having Clark in their networks. Not all stories end up like Clark's. Finding a job can be difficult and even frustrating at times. However, Clark's story illustrates the point that being aware of the networks you are already a part of can make the process less difficult. Clark also learned the importance of gaining new network connections. Most networks are made up of people who share a

DEGREES OF NETWORKING

A great thing about your network is that it doesn't consist of only people you know. Think about all of your friends on Facebook or your followers on Instagram. Those people are part of your network. But your friends' friends and followers are also connected to you. They are simply one degree removed. These one-step-removed relationships can be even more helpful in real life than on social media. For instance, your aunt Cynthia's friend is a lawyer, a career you're interested in knowing more about. Your aunt can help connect the two of you. Ta da! Your network just grew a whole bunch.

desire to succeed and improve their lives. But how to get started? By taking a closer look at networks, it will be easier to understand what makes them so valuable when planning your career.

MAINTAINING AND GROWING YOUR NETWORK

Networking is an important component of just about every business or profession. As Clark's example showed, however, networks do not always involve work or business associates. People are all part of one or more networks that develop naturally the longer they know others and the more individuals they meet. Family and friends are the easiest type of network to develop. However, people also build networking relationships with those they meet at houses of worship, while playing sports, in their community, and online. Networking is the way people take advantage of the connections they share.

Growing a network requires effort and organization. You can't simply make a new friend and wait for him or her to offer you a job. You need to be persistent in reminding people of your connection. You also need to be able to recognize an opportunity when one pops up and be bold enough to act on that opportunity before it slips away.

When networking, you will rely on the communication skills you are learning in school. Good writing skills are essential. You will need to write introduction emails, thank-you letters, summaries, notes, and so on. Good speaking skills are just as vital. You need to be able to make a positive impression on people when talking in person, on the phone, and online.

Networking is a lifelong process. As your networks grow over time, so does your quality of life. Learning to make the most of your acquaintances will enable you to accomplish more and go further. A strong network does not appear overnight. It requires time to develop relationships with people and act on leads. It also requires clear goals and realistic planning. The harder you work at networking, the easier it will get, and the better you will get at it.

The bigger your network, the greater the chance of getting what you want when you really need it. But don't forget that you have to be willing to give a favor before you get a favor. Networking is a two-way street.

MYTHS & FACTS

MYTH: You have to be outgoing to be good at networking.
FACT: Not good at talking to strangers about yourself? That's OK!
So much of networking is capitalizing on who you already know,
and it's not scary to talk to them, right? So chat up your neighbor
who has a cool job, and find out how she got there. Or ask your
brother's best friend what it's like studying his major in college.
Be curious about the people in your life and—voila!—you're
networking.

MYTH: Networking is about getting something you want.
FACT: Networking is not just about getting a job, a grant or
scholarship, or anything in particular. The major benefit of
networking is the network itself. Basically, networking is meeting a
person and forming a connection that may someday benefit both of
you. It is about sharing information, knowledge, and other contacts.
A contact is someone you befriend before you even need his or her
help. Most network contacts are mutually beneficial—that is, both
individuals can gain something from the friendship. Networking is
all about making smart contacts and knowing that they may help
you someday.

MYTH: Networking is awkward.
FACT: Networking can be awkward, but it shouldn't be. Networking
is simply about connecting with people who have similar interests,
and you probably already do that in all parts of your life, maybe
without even realizing it. Are you on a team or in a club? Do you
and your friends have a favorite book or movie series? You're
connecting via a shared interest. Networking is the same concept,
except because it's about work, it can get a bad rap.

GETTING READY TO NETWORK

To network, you must be able to clearly communicate your ideas and goals. It's also a great idea to get your online profile set up and looking professional. Consider these the tools you need to network successfully.

FINDING YOUR VOICE

Before you can reap the benefits of networking, you need to talk to others and build friendships. Getting practice talking and listening to others—face to face—is the best way to develop good conversational skills.

IMPRESS WITH YOUR BEST

First impressions are important. Most people form an opinion about you within ten seconds. Eye contact is important. Frequently ask yourself what color the other person's eyes are. Be aware of how you are standing and where your hands are. Slouching and shoving

It can be nerve-racking to meet for a networking coffee, but you can do it. Brainstorm some conversation topics ahead of time and make sure to be on time. With preparation, you will impress.

your hands in your pockets can make you seem shy or annoyed. Shifting from foot to foot can make you seem anxious or nervous. Speak clearly when introducing yourself. When someone asks you a question, try to answer with more than just a few words.

CONVERSATION 101

When first meeting someone, always keep the conversation simple, and speak in a manner the listener will understand. Never start a conversation by stating what it is you hope to get from the other person.

Instead, introduce yourself and try to find a topic that both of you will enjoy discussing.

It is a good idea to relate something personal about yourself when meeting someone new. But it is not a good idea to get too personal or to dominate the conversation with stories about yourself. A conversation requires talking and listening. It is good to talk about yourself, but it is bad to dominate a conversation. When you ask a question, wait for the answer. Don't talk over the other person, finish another speaker's sentence, or interrupt. A good rule is to wait three seconds after someone has finished speaking before responding.

Try to be an active listener. Nod to show agreement without interrupting the speaker. Do not play with pens or papers while someone else is talking. Pay attention not only to the speaker's words but also to body language, which sometimes reveals more than words do. Active listeners reflect back what they have heard to get confirmation that they have understood the speaker correctly.

Remain objective. Stay focused on the speaker and hear him or her out, rather than allowing your emotions to take over. Take time to observe and analyze what the speaker is saying. This step will ultimately help you to interact with the speaker in a manner that is beneficial to you both.

Without fully knowing a person, it is impossible to tell what he or she might find uninteresting or even offensive. After two or three conversations, you will be better able to decide which topics are OK to discuss and which are off-limits. For example, people can disagree on religious topics, and it is usually best to avoid them on a first meeting. On the other hand, if you meet someone at your church, temple, or mosque or on a religious retreat, talking about religious topics may be the best way to get to know the person. Use your best judgment and be polite.

ONLINE ACCESS

The internet gives you access to the entire world, making it an amazing networking resource. But it can also be completely overwhelming. So how best to maximize the World Wide Web? By making your online presence work for you. Though it may take some time to get organized, the internet can be a great way to make new connections. Just be mindful, as always, about whom you are sharing info with online. Considering making your privacy settings so that only friends and friends of friends can see your pages. And never ever put any personal info online, like your address.

GET SOCIAL

Adults are so often telling kids to get off their phones, but networking is one instance in which social media can be a great tool. Think about what kind of field you are interested in, and consider curating your social media feeds to reflect that. For example, you love business and would like to work in the corporate world one day. You can retweet business articles—that you have read in full, not just the headline—with a smart, insightful comment of your own. Are you doing a school project that shows off your skills? Take a picture and post it.

In addition to the content that you provide, consider your list of followers. Follow some local entrepreneurs you admire, or maybe the authors of some business books you've enjoyed. Look at who those people follow and see if you find any of them interesting. If you do,

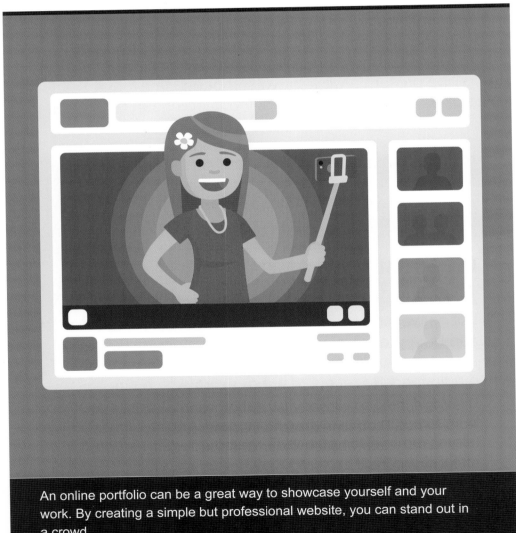

An online portfolio can be a great way to showcase yourself and your work. By creating a simple but professional website, you can stand out in a crowd.

consider following those people as well. Comment on their posts from time to time. They might reply, and you can strike up a relationship. "Eventually, you can say you would love to work for them," prolific Twitter user and bestselling author Aliza Licht told Anna Cooperberg at Teen Vogue. "If you've demonstrated you can be excited about their work and professional at the same time, they just might call you in!"

PORTFOLIO POWER

Another great way to showcase yourself and enhance your digital academic footprint is to create your own website. It can be a simple design, using readily available free templates. (But if HTML is your thing, make your website as advanced as you'd like—show off those skills!) Search for website examples in the field you're interested in. Look at what the people you follow on social media have on their websites. This information will give you good ideas for what your website should look like. The key is for your website to reflect who you are and where you want to go.

Perhaps you'd like to study art. An online portfolio, showcasing a few of your favorite pieces that you've created, a short "about me" paragraph, and your email and social media handles are all you need. If you'd like, you can then list your website on your social media accounts. Or list your URL at the bottom of emails. When you send your networking emails, people can click through to learn more about you if they'd like.

SOCIAL MEDIA SAFETY

You've probably heard this before, but it's so important that it bears repeating. Make sure to keep your social media feed full of appropriate content. Selfies are OK, and so are pictures of you and your friends having fun. But you should not include alcohol, drugs, or sexual content. (And no private information either, like your home address, name of your school, Social Security number, or credit card numbers. Make sure that you've checked your privacy settings on your social media accounts.) Employers, college recruiters, and maybe even your grandma are all looking you up online. When you're working to build your network, you want to showcase your best self. That means prioritizing a social media presence that highlights why someone would want to talk with you, and maybe even work with you.

Licht also told Teen Vogue, "Anything you put online is fair game for an employer to review. The way I think of it is, if I were a reporter writing about myself and I was Googling myself to do it, what would that article look like? What pictures would I pull? With the advent of social media, the walls are gone. The screen shot is more powerful than the delete button."

Social media can be a great networking tool. But be sure your presence is professional.

THE POWER OF THE PEN

When building a successful network, persuasive writing can be a powerful asset. On the other hand, frequent grammatical and spelling errors may convince a potential employer or network contact that you are not worth doing business with. Be sure to read your text over at least once, and use spell-check—but don't rely on it, it can make mistakes, too. Have a friend or parent look over an important email before you hit Send.

A well-written email can help you get a meeting with someone you've been unable to connect with. It could also convince a potential business partner to work with you. An appropriate follow-up email, maybe a week or so later, can remind employers and contacts that you are eager and capable. A handwritten thank-you note after a meeting can also make a great impression. These tactics can all help you to stand out in a crowd.

When penning an email to a potential contact or employer, be mindful of what tone and language you use. Depending on the context, the email will contain different types of information. A letter of application will sound different from the cover letter of a résumé. Be careful to write a letter appropriate for its purpose.

YOUR RÉSUMÉ

A résumé, sometimes called a CV (short for "curriculum vitae"), is a standard part of any application for employment. All high school graduates should know how to write a solid résumé. You might think you don't have enough experience to create one, but all it really takes is one or two previous jobs and a high school education. Résumés are a place to record this

Your résumé should showcase your skills and experiences in a clean and easy-to-read fashion. Choose a template like this one to best list why you are the person for the job.

information in bite-sized chunks for potential employers to get a better understanding of your employment and educational histories. In addition, résumés often include a summary of your knowledge base and career aspirations.

The purpose of a résumé is to get an interview. Essentially, the résumé is your first contact with an employer. To make a great first impression, your résumé needs to be well written and professionally composed. Your résumé will evolve and change over time, but it should always follow a clean, structured format.

GET LINKED UP

As you go about getting your professional online presence set up, you may want to consider creating a LinkedIn profile. LinkedIn is a social media website where your profile page is your résumé. The site now accepts users ages thirteen and up. *Forbes* magazine reports that some colleges consider a prospective student's LinkedIn profile when determining admissions. Schools also have profiles under the site's University Pages, where you can learn about local alumni—more potential networking connections. Using LinkedIn's site and search engine be a great way to try to establish some relationships. So polish that résumé and think about getting it online. With a professional-looking profile picture, you'll be ready to jump-start your network ASAP.

Now you know all the tools you'll need to get your network started. You're ready to get to it!

BUILDING YOUR NETWORK

So who, exactly, is in your network? Probably more people than you might think. The trick is to home in on those who can really help you get where you'd like to be.

THANKS, MOM

Family and friends are your closest network connections. Parents, best friends, aunts and uncles, and grandparents often help people get their first jobs while they are in high school or right after graduation.

For example, take Sara. She has just graduated from high school. She has been filling out applications around town but hasn't found a job yet. Sara's mother, Ellen, works for a local flower shop. Ellen asks her boss, Caroline, if there is anything Sara can do around the shop to earn some money. Caroline mentions that one of her flower suppliers has been looking for a new employee. Sara goes to apply for the job at the greenhouse right away. The owner, Winston, says that

Ready to network but not sure where to start? Ask parents or trusted adults. They can share access to their network to get you started.

Caroline recommended her for the position. After a short interview, Sara gets the job!

In this example, Ellen did not actually get her daughter the greenhouse job. However, Ellen did prove to be a valuable network connection. Through Ellen, Sara earned two new connections—Caroline, who recommended her for the greenhouse job, and Winston, who ultimately hired her. It is important to note that this is how all networks function, not just family-and-friend networks. It is a game of give and take with the people you know and the people they know.

SCHOOL TIES

The relationships people form with teachers, coaches, and principals are not usually the same as those they share with friends and family. It can sometimes be difficult for them to give individual students attention. Still, teachers and coaches typically want to help young people succeed in life. Teachers may be happy to give you advice about colleges or jobs. They may even have connections with people in a career that interests you. Coaches may also be able to give you advice or put you in contact with an employer.

Schools sometimes have career counselors on staff who can help you establish professional network connections. School guidance counselors can help you prepare for college or employment. They

can also help you to build your network by pointing you in the right direction. Guidance counselors can tell you about job fairs, college tours, employment agencies, military recruiters, and more.

Academic networking can extend beyond high school. If you decide to attend college, you will meet more people who will make great network connections:

Teachers, coaches, guidance counselors, and more can help you build your network. All you have to do is ask.

professors, instructors, resident assistants, academic advisers, other students, and so on. You may also take continuing education courses once you have graduated from high school. There, too, you will have opportunities to meet plenty of people who are potential network contacts.

A GUIDING HAND

As you build your network, you might find someone whom you would like to have as your mentor. A mentor is someone who watches over the progress of less experienced people and fosters their development. Mentors are often older than the people they help, but that is not always the case. They don't have to be older than you—just more experienced. Mentors are people who share their time, knowledge, and experience with someone who is just starting down a similar career path.

So how do you find a mentor? You might find a mentor in your family, at school, at your house of worship, or on a sports team. You may also meet one at work as you begin to establish a career.

Another great way to find a mentor is to use your network. "Find some common ground with whoever you are reaching out to—fellow alums of a school or members of a professional or personal organization, or similar career paths," Shannon Otto, director of global social media for Clinique told Mandi Woodruff at Teen Vogue.

Write a short email introducing yourself and showing that you know whom you're emailing. Remember how important your business writing is, and make that first impression count.

Like networking, a mentorship should go both ways. Tracy Sun, cofounder of Poshmark, told Woodruff:

> I don't like when people ask me to be their mentor, and expect me to do all the work. I love when people reach out to me and ask, but they need to be thoughtful in doing so. It's just as much about what a mentee can teach a mentor—sharing new perspectives and teaching new experience as it is about what a mentor can teach you. When this is understood, I know it's a great match.

Not everyone will have a mentor. As with all endeavors in life, you can rely on others for support, but you should be prepared to grapple with problems on your own. In any case, a mentor—should you be fortunate enough to find one—can be a powerful network ally.

GET OUT THERE

Now that you have a better idea of who is already in your network, you need to consider ways of branching out and finding new network connections. There are many ways to meet new people who share your interests and desires to expand your networking sphere.

One of the most effective and natural ways of expanding your network is to socialize. It's important

A great networking resource is your local library. Check for teen or student programs online, or visit the library in person and talk with a librarian.

to put down your phone, step away from your laptop, and spend some time talking to people face to face. It may sound scary but it is worth it. Anytime you meet and converse with people, you increase the potential of establishing a network connection. Always try to meet at least three new people every time you attend a social function. Chances are at least one of them will prove to be helpful to you in some way.

Consider checking out what your local library has to offer. Some libraries offer programs where you can learn about different professions you may not have even considered. In North Carolina, librarians Amy Wyckoff and Marie Harris had a photographer, a tattoo artist, a pharmacy technician, and a skateboard shop owner come to talk to interested local teens. As they explained in their article in *American Libraries,* "The library has access to so many useful resources to help teens learn about career paths ... We can also help [teens] find information about internships, camps, and other educational programs—anything that can set them on the path toward a fulfilling career."

Joining a club, organization, or association can be a great way to meet new network contacts. Everyone has an interest, hobby, or pastime. Whatever you like to call it, just about every activity has an organization or association dedicated to people who enjoy it. There are business associations, sports organizations, men's and women's clubs, even associations for dog lovers. Many people with whom you share a common interest will be just as happy to add you to their network as you will be to add them to yours.

A business card can be a great asset to have while networking. Choose an eye-catching but easy-to-read format like these pictured here. Search for templates online and find one that represents you.

THE POWER OF THE GROUP

Many serious networkers are members of one or more networking groups. You can find out about these groups online, either via a simple internet search, by checking sites like Eventbrite and Meetup, or by looking at social media on topics you are interested in exploring.

These groups meet at regular intervals to talk and exchange information and leads. This meeting might occur once a week, once a month, or a few times a

THE BUSINESS OF BUSINESS CARDS

Business cards for teens? Why not! You can certainly trade phones to take someone's info, but at a professional event like a job fair or networking meetup, handing out business cards can put you a step ahead. A business card should have your name, phone number, email address, website address, or social media handles (assuming your content is aimed toward finding a job). Pick a design that reflects who you are, but remember, you are aiming for a professional look, so don't select a design that is too wild or busy. Your main objective is to hand out your contact information to potential networking contacts, so the cards need to be easy to read. Business cards do not have to be expensive. Look around online—check reviews to find somewhere reputable—or call a print shop in your town.

year. The makeup and rules of networking groups vary. Some groups are for people from the same industry. Others allow only one person from a given industry or job position at a time to avoid conflicts between members vying for the same leads and referrals. Some groups have no restrictions on membership. Others require members to pay fees. Fees help guarantee that a member will not back out, and they help to pay for meeting costs, learning materials, and guest speakers.

The more frequently network groups meet, the stronger their network connections grow. If you can afford to join one, the benefits may be worth the membership fees. Keep in mind that group networkers are usually very serious about the meeting. You will be expected to contribute to discussions and share leads when appropriate.

JOB FAIRS, HEADHUNTERS, AND MORE

There are other ways to expand your network. One is by attending a job fair. Employers set up booths or tables, and potential employees can stop by to chat and drop off their résumé or a business card with their contact information. Everyone you'd meet at a job fair is a potential network contact. Another plus is that it is easy to find people with the same interests at a job fair.

Some companies employ headhunters—human resources employees who search for the best person for a position. Headhunters are always excellent additions to your network. You often have to pay for their service, but it can be worth it.

Although you would probably like to think of it as your last choice, you can also network to find employment at the unemployment office. Unemployment offices are connected to statewide databases filled with leads and job offers. Most also have career counselors and job training classes. These outlets offer you a place to go to look for a job, but they also offer you a chance to strengthen your network.

There are so many ways for you to grow your network once you really start to think about it. Every time you step out the door is an opportunity to meet someone new.

GET NETWORKING AND SET THOSE GOALS

S o you're ready to network. You established a connection on Twitter. You sent your introductory email. Your persistence and professionalism has paid off, and you're meeting a potential network connection for coffee. Now what?

TALKING POINTS

The good news is that you know this meeting is coming, so you have time to prepare. It is always best to plan ahead if you have the time. A well-thought-out strategy will keep you focused on your goals in networking, in your career, and in life. In her book *Networking for Everyone,* L. Michelle Tullier says: "Like any endeavor in life, it's important to have a plan when you are preparing to network. Otherwise, there's no telling where you'll end up or how long it will take to get there."

You probably know some information about your potential contact, but it's good to do some research, maybe a quick internet search—though not so much as

Preparing before a networking meeting is always a good idea. Looking up whom you will be meeting with shows you are interested. Be polite and let your personality shine. You will do great.

to veer into creepy territory. Remember how doing your homework can help in finding a mentor? It's the same here. People are flattered when you take the time to learn about them, showing that you're prepared.

Think of some questions you'd like to ask. What do you want to know about your contact? Remember your conversational skills. Don't dominate the conversation, but do participate.

BE PREPARED

You should always be ready to take advantage of new networking opportunities—planned and unplanned. When at a party or school event, try to talk to some new people. You never know, they might be able to help you build your network. At the very least, it's good practice to talk with new and different people. By frequently meeting new people, you improve your conversational skills and increase your network. This action will increase your chances of achieving your goals.

REMEMBER TO FOLLOW UP

After you have met a new network contact, don't neglect him or her. Even if there is nothing the person can do for you right now, keep the lines of communication open. You may establish a valuable friendship with this person simply by emailing him or her occasionally. Then again, there might be something you can do for the other person, which will strengthen your connection. It's always nice having people in your network who "owe you one"!

It's common for people in your network to offer you a lead. This is the name or number of someone who might be able to help you. When you are given a lead, promptly contact that person. And when you are contacted by a referral, be ready to take advantage of the situation. Don't allow these types of opportunities to slip away—they are exactly the reason you are networking in the first place. Likewise, never forget to follow up with people whom you have already contacted. Be on time for meetings, and send a thank-you letter after meeting with an important person. Although you don't want to pester or annoy a potential

Always remember to write a short thank-you email after a networking meeting. Someone took the time to speak with you, so express your thanks.

network contact, you certainly don't want that person to forget about you.

KNOW YOUR GOALS

When networking, it is in your best interest to present yourself as a competent, motivated individual. You need to convince others that you are worth their time and that you have something to contribute to the relationship. To properly "sell" yourself to potential employers and network connections, you need to know what it is you want and how you plan to get it. You can achieve this goal by strategizing.

In all of your endeavors, goals serve as signposts of the things you want to achieve. Networking won't help

THE ELEVATOR PITCH

It's a great idea to have a few sentences prepared about yourself, in case you get nervous, or if there's only a small opening in a conversation. Think specifically about what your goals are. Are you looking for a job? A connection to a school you're applying to? To learn more about a certain career? In the most basic structure, you can say who you are, where you go to school, what you're interested in and why. Add in details relevant to what you hope to achieve. Practice in front of a mirror or for a parent or friend so you're ready.

you achieve much if you're not sure of where you want to go. Keeping these signposts in front of you as you work toward them keeps you motivated and focused on the results of your efforts. Your goals reflect who you are and what you want to achieve.

Having clear goals makes it more likely that your network will produce positive results. They can be short-term goals ("Introduce myself to Fred Lewis at the next town meeting and get his phone number"). Or they can be long-term goals ("Get the permits and funding

Having an idea of where you want to go will help you get there. By planning out your goals, you are more likely to achieve success.

needed to open a bookstore in town"). Either way, you need to look at the size and scope of your goals and make sure they are possible. Your goals need to be ambitious but realistic. Be aware that your goals may change over time. When this change happens, you need to reassess what you want to accomplish and then revise your goals accordingly.

NAMING OBJECTIVES

Goals are a picture of the future as you hope it will be. Your goals, especially long-term goals, may sometimes seem out of reach. However, it is important to remember that reaching your goals doesn't just happen—you need to work at it one step at a time. You can accomplish your goals by setting objectives. Objectives are smaller goals you accomplish on your way to achieving your main goals. If goals are signposts, then objectives can be thought of as mile markers.

As with goals, objectives must be carefully planned when strategizing. For example, your goal is to become a world-famous rock star. That's a great goal, but it might be nothing more than a pipe dream if you don't plan out the objectives needed to reach that goal. These objectives would include the following: learn to play an instrument well, find other musicians to start a band, rent studio time, record some music and put it up on YouTube, get a manager/agent, and so on. In this way, all of your goals can be broken down into smaller goals called objectives.

MAKING A PLAN

Once you have mapped out your goals and objectives, it is time to make a plan for how you will go about achieving them. Ask yourself what you need to do to reach your objectives. The activities that you come up with will become part of your plan. The beginning steps of your plan may include researching a topic online. It will also include networking with people who can help you reach your goals.

Goals and objectives represent the big picture. They state what it is you hope to achieve and the steps required to get there. Plans, however, need to be more detailed. Your plan is a list of actions that will help make your goals reality. Write your plans down. Try to establish exact dates and specific contacts, and then stick to them. Create a plan that is both interesting to you and capable of producing results. Think about what you can do by yourself, as well as whom you can turn to for help and guidance along the way. Ideally, your plan will also enable you to meet many new people, some of whom will turn out to be valuable network contacts.

Sometimes, plans can be overly ambitious or they may be misguided. By doing a little research, you can be sure your plans will be appropriate. Before jotting down an idea for a plan, make sure it is doable by researching the possible methods and outcomes. Once you are sure your plans are practical and possible, write them down or type them out. Then it's time to act.

Once you have a strong grasp of who you are and what you have to offer, then you can begin to network effectively. Know whom you're talking with, what you want to ask that person, and what you hope to gain from the conversation. Although network relationships are a two-way street, don't be afraid to tell others about your aspirations and strengths. These details will help get you noticed, which is important when strengthening and extending your network.

10 GREAT QUESTIONS

TO ASK A NETWORK CONNECTION

1. Why did you decide on this career?
2. What type of education did you get?
3. What do you think I should do to succeed?
4. What do you wish you'd known before you started in your career?
5. What attributes do you think make you great at your job?
6. What do you most look for in an employee?
7. What is the one thing you want everyone to know about your career?
8. What's the most important piece of advice you would tell someone considering your career?
9. What's the best and the worst part of your job?
10. What do you want to do next?

YOU FOUND A JOB! NOW WHAT?

Congratulations! You've found a job! But don't give up on networking just yet. Networking can still do a lot more for you. Getting a job is a great accomplishment, but it is only the first step. There is so much that will happen in your career as you continue to grow. Your goals will mature and shift, and your network can help you adapt to all of these changes.

KEEPING UP WITH YOUR NETWORK

Once you have formed a network, it is important to maintain connections. But how do you tend to your network if you aren't actively relying on your contacts as job-finding resources?

Email your network contacts from time to time, just to say hello and find out what's new. Maybe send along a link to an article you read that you think they might enjoy. If you're finishing up with an internship or job, be sure to check back in from time to time with a quick email. "Very few interns bother to do this, but those

You worked hard networking, and it paid off. You are ready to succeed at work, but don't forget to keep your network nourished, too.

who do really stand out, and often develop professional relationships that serve them well long into their careers," writer Alison Green told Anna Cooperberg at Teen Vogue.

Also be sure to volunteer your help any way you can. When people call you for advice or a favor, it is in your best interest to do what you can for them. Returning the favor is a great way to guarantee that people in your network will be there for you the next time you need them. Some contacts you will end up seeing on a regular basis, which will make it easier for you to help one another.

THE POWER OF THE THANK-YOU NOTE

If someone in your network helped you find a job, it is a good idea to send a handwritten thank-you note. Emails are always nice, but putting something in the mail is an extra special touch that can let your contact know that you really appreciated their time and assistance. Some may go as far as to include a small gift, like a coffee shop gift card, but that is not necessary. It is important to simply acknowledge how that person helped you. This expression of appreciation can also help to strengthen your networking relationship.

As you mature in your role as a networker, however, you may start to be a bit more discerning about whom you include in your network. You will come to realize that not all people make good network connections. You may run into a few people who are not interested in the give-and-take aspects of networking. These types do everything for themselves. They may accept a favor from you one day and refuse to return it the next. In time, you'll figure out how to distinguish the few selfish networkers from the majority of sharing networkers.

DETERMINING YOUR CAREER PATH

Just because you have found a job doesn't mean that you will be in that position for the rest of your life. Some people begin working for a company or organization and decide to stay with it for the long haul. Perhaps they get promoted and receive raises on a regular basis and don't see the point in searching for a new job. However, other people may feel the need to move to another company or even a new line of work. This feeling is common when a worker is bored or in search of a better salary or when a company is laying off personnel.

COOPERATIVE COWORKERS

Once you have a job, the network connections that you have will still be of value to you. Then, as you work at your job, you will begin to add a whole new layer of network contacts to your list. The longer you are at

Now that you have a job, you've got a whole new set of network connections: your coworkers.

your job, the more people you will meet, and the more contacts you will be able to add to your network. These might include coworkers, managers, clients, and so on. It may also include people who visit your place of work occasionally, such as couriers and other service providers. Most business contacts are sure to help you out in a time of need, especially when they work with you on a frequent basis.

You may find yourself in a job one day where networking is just as important as other skills. Salespeople who work on commission, for example, usually spend as much time networking as they do selling. When not making a sale, they are making connections with people, which will increase the chances that they will make a sale in the future. The connections you make with other businesspeople may benefit you for the length of your career or longer.

THINKING AHEAD

Once you have determined what career path you want to follow, you tend to meet and befriend the types of people who can help you as you travel that path. These are people who can get you interviews with new companies or let you know when they will be hiring.

For example, Alicia takes photographs of children and families for a local department store. She likes her job, but she thinks she could make more money and have more fun working elsewhere. Alicia decides to do some networking. She calls an art teacher who used to be her instructor to ask for tips on searching for photography jobs. She calls a friend to help her write a résumé. Last, she calls a former employer who now works for a major US newspaper. Alicia is making good use of her network to further her career. Simply knowing someone doesn't guarantee that you will get a job based on a recommendation. However, network connections often help get your foot in the door.

RESIGNING RESPECTFULLY

Suppose that your networking was successful, and you find a better job. Even when leaving a company, it is wise to do so in a professional manner. Remaining on good terms with former bosses, managers, and coworkers will guarantee that many of them will remain in your network in the future. On the other hand, "burning bridges" before leaving for your new

Networking is a skill you will develop over your entire life. By thinking strategically and helping others, you are off to a great start.

job will certainly reduce the number of people in your network. Always give at least two weeks' notice when leaving a job, and do your best to make the transition a smooth one for everybody. If you are asked to give an exit interview, be as courteous and complimentary as possible. You never know, down the road, if you may be able to benefit from the people you are leaving behind.

Networking is a lifelong process. The more you do it, the better you get at it. You will continue to benefit from your network in many ways, as long as you maintain it. Over time, you will develop the ability to see how people can fit into your network or identify those who you don't want in your network at all.

Don't be afraid to jump right in and start networking. Go out and meet three new people today. One of those people might prove to be your greatest network ally.

ally A person who provides help or support to another.

ambitious Wanting to achieve something specific.

application A standard form many employers require when one applies for a job. Potential employees must provide basic information, including home address, previous experience, and education.

competent Having the ability to do a task well.

curriculum vitae A listing of one's jobs, experiences, and education.

database An organized set of computerized data.

discerning Discriminating or selective.

endeavor Real, determined effort to accomplish something.

e-tailer A method of selling goods or services online.

exit interview A meeting when one is leaving a job to discuss one's experiences.

headhunter A human resources employee tasked with finding new employees for job openings.

HTML Hypertext Markup Language, the language used to create websites.

motivated Having the desire to accomplish an objective or goal.

mutual Having the same feelings toward each other.

persuasive Working to convince someone of something, via argument and the presentation of facts.

potential With a possibility of occurring some time later.

referral Someone who does business with another person thanks to the recommendation of a third party.

résumé A typed record of a person's education, employment experience, and career objective, often used when applying to jobs.

vocational school A school where students are trained in a trade or skill that may be used when pursuing a career.

BNI Canada
Website: http://www.bnicanada.ca
Facebook and Twitter: @BNI_Canada
The Canadian version of BNI has many networking
    chapters and resources.

Business Network International (BNI)
545 College Commerce Way
Upland, CA 91786
(800) 825-8286
Email: bni@bni.com
Website: http://www.bni.com
Facebook: @BNIOfficialPage
Twitter: @BNI_official_pg
BNI is referred to as the "World's Largest Referral
    Organization." Members get access to newsletters,
    workshops, job boards, and more.

CareerOneStop
(877) US2-JOBS
Email: info@CareerOneStop.org
Website: http://www.careeronestop.org
Facebook: @CareerOneStop.org
Twitter: @Career1Stop
The US federal government's website has many resources
    to help with career planning and job searching,
    including résumé help and career assessments.

Career Planning and Adult Development Network
PO Box 611930
San Jose, CA 95161-1930
(408) 559-4946

Website: http://www.careernetwork.org

This networking organization connects teens and career counselors. There are articles on job hunting, a newsletter, and more resources to help teens with their job search and career path.

Professional Association of Résumé Writers & Career Coaches (PARW/CC)

1388 Brightwaters Boulevard NE

St. Petersburg, FL 33704

(800) 822-7279

Email: PARWhq@aol.com

Website: http://www.parw.com

Those in search of résumé help or professional career coaches can find a great deal of helpful information here.

Small Business Owners & Professionals Association

30 Intermodal Drive, Unit # 6

Brampton, ON L6T 5K1

Canada

(866) 678-1385

Email: info@sboapa.org

Website: http://www.sboapa.org

This Canadian nonprofit organization was created to help small business owners and their employees succeed. Networking events and membership benefits are available.

Carter, Linda, and Tina Cargile. *What I Need 2 Succeed: From A to Z for Teens*. New York, NY: Morgan James Publishing, 2016.

Christen, Carol, and Richard N. Bolles. *What Color Is Your Parachute? For Teens: Discover Yourself, Design Your Future*. Emeryville, CA: Ten Speed Press, 2015.

Criswell, Patti K., and Angela Martini. *Knowing What to Say: Finding the Words to Fit Any Situation*. Middleton, WI: American Girl Publishing, 2018.

Furgang, Adam. *20 Great Career-Building Activities Using YouTube*. New York, NY: Rosen Publishing, 2017.

Henneberg, Susan. *Step-by-Step Guide to Effective Job Hunting & Career Preparedness*. New York, NY: Rosen Publishing, 2015.

Lew, Kristi. *20 Great Career-Building Activities Using Pinterest*. New York, NY: Rosen Publishing, 2017.

McGuire, Kara. *All About the Green: The Teen's Guide to Finding Work and Making Money*. North Mankato, MN: Compass Point, 2015.

Rodriguez, Joshua. *Embracing the Awkward: A Guide for Teens to Succeed at School, Life, and Relationships*. Coral Gables, FL: Mango Publishing, 2018.

Singh, Lilly. *How to Be a Bawse: A Guide to Conquering Life*. London, UK: Penguin Random House, 2017.

Skeen, Michelle. *Communication Skills for Teens: How to Listen, Express & Connect for Success*. Oakland, CA: Instant Help Books, 2016.

Arruda, William. "Why Parents Should Help Their Teens Use LinkedIn." *Forbes*. Retrieved February 20, 2019. https://www.forbes.com/sites /williamarruda/2017/07/18/why-parents-should-help -their-teens-use-linkedin/#6fb6d52541e1.

Cooperberg, Anna. "The One Career Trick You Need to Know Now: Networking." *Teen Vogue*. June 28, 2013. https://www.teenvogue.com/story/how-to -network.

Crispin, Gerry, and Mark Mehler. *CareerXroads*. Kendall Park, NJ: MMC Group, 2003.

Darling, Diane. *The Networking Survival Guide: Get the Success You Want by Tapping into the People You Know*. New York, NY: McGraw-Hill, 2003.

Enelow, Wendy S., and Shelly Goldman. *Insider's Guide to Finding a Job*. St. Paul, MN: Jist Publishing, 2005.

Kerr, Cherie. *Networking Skills That Will Get You the Job You Want*. Cincinnati, OH: Betterway Books, 1999.

Kramer, Marc. *Power Networking*. Chicago, IL: VGM Career Horizons, 1998.

Mait, Josh. "The 7 Biggest Networking Myths, Busted." *Inc.*, October 23, 2015. https://www.inc.com/josh -mait/the-7-biggest-networking-myths-busted.html.

Moore, Alexa-Jane. "The Dos and Don'ts of Student Networking." *Guardian*, June 18, 2014. https://www. theguardian.com/education/2014/jun/18 /student-guide-to-networking-graduate-jobs.

Tugend, Alina. "If a Teenager Lands a Summer Job, the Value Is Lasting." *New York Times,* June 13, 2014. https://www.nytimes.com/2014/06/14/your-money /For-Teenagers-Summer-Jobs-Are-Valuable.html.

Tullier, L. Michelle. *Networking for Everyone! Connecting with People for Career and Job Success.* St. Paul, MN: Jist Publishing, 1998.

Tullier, L. Michelle. *Networking for Job Search and Career Success.* St. Paul, MN: Jist Publishing, 2004.

Woodruff, Mandi. "How to Find a Mentor." *Teen Vogue*, January 31, 2017. https://www.teenvogue.com/story/how-to-find-a-mentor-dos-donts.

Wyckoff, Amy, and Marie Harris. "Career Workshops for Teens: Bringing in professionals to talk with young adults." *American Libraries,* November 1, 2018. https://americanlibrariesmagazine.org/2018/11/01/career-workshops-for-teens.

INDEX

A
active listener, 18
ally, network, 31, 54

B
business cards, 4, 35, 36

C
careers
    aspirations, 25, 50–54
    challenge, 8
    connections, 13, 28, 47
    counselors, 28, 37
    importance of networking in
        any, 4, 9, 13, 30, 33, 38, 42,
        48–49
    taking charge of, 7
coaches, 4, 28
communication skills, 14, 16,
    40
conversational skills, 16,
    17–19, 40
counselors, 28, 29, 37
coworkers, 51–52, 53

D
databases, 37

E
elevator pitch, 42
exit interview, 54

F
family connections, 8, 12,
13–14, 26, 28, 30

G
goals, 5, 8, 14, 16, 38, 40, 44,
    45, 48
    knowing your, 42–44
    long-term, 43, 44
groups, networking, 35–36

H
headhunters, 36–37

I
interviews, 4, 11, 25, 28, 52, 54

J
job fairs, 29, 35, 36–37

L
lead, 14, 35, 36, 37, 40
library, 33
LinkedIn, 25

M
managers, 11, 44, 52, 53
mentor, 30, 31, 39

O
objectives, 35, 44, 45
offer, job, 4, 11, 14, 37
online presence, 7, 19–21
opportunities, 5, 14, 30, 37,
    40–41

ABOUT THE AUTHORS

Elissa Thompson is a journalist who has been published in *USA Weekend*, the *Baltimore Sun*, and *In Touch Weekly*, among other publications. She received her master's in journalism from the University of Maryland. She has written and edited other books for Rosen Publishing, a position she got via networking.

Greg Roza is a writer and editor specializing in library books and educational materials. He lives in Hamburg, New York, with his wife, Abigail; his son, Lincoln; and his daughters, Autumn and Daisy. Roza has a master's degree in English from SUNY Fredonia. To this day, he continues to use networking to strengthen his career.

PHOTO CREDITS